Lacy Sunshine's Enchanted Kingdom Coloring Book

by Heather Valentin

MW00877774

Lacy Sunshine
presents....

An exclusive sneak peek to

Heather Valentin's Upcoming Coloring
Book and New Character
Collection....

Dragon Flower Pot Hatchlings!

Coming Soon!

Meet Dragemma and Dragaisy.
Enjoy!

Heather Valentin

www.lacysunshine.weebly.com

51299053R00040

Made in the USA
San Bernardino, CA
18 July 2017